"I've never had so much fun reading a professional book, ever. Somehow each chapter is equal parts hilarious, gleeful, inspiring and practical. I would recommend this to every educator I know and even parents and students. This is a book you can come back to again and again to laugh, learn and Make each time in a new way." — Jennie Magiera, Educator and Author of *Courageous Edventures*

"*Your Starter Guide to Makerspaces* makes any Hufflepuff feel like they can tackle the Maker movement with the brains of a Ravenclaw, the confidence of a Gryffindor, and the cleverness of a Slytherin." — Emily Gover, Spirit Animal, Edtech Nerd and Librarian

"In *Your Starter Guide to Makerspaces*, Nicholas Provenzano creates a practical and personal look at how to get started with the Maker mind-set. Chock full of nerdtastic pop culture references, the book practices what it preaches and even invites the reader to make content and hack the book itself. While not taking itself too seriously, this book serves up some seriously useful content and new ideas on Makerspaces." — Adam Bellow, Co-Founder Breakout EDU

"Interested in STEAM education and even starting a Makerspace in your community? Then this book should be on your reading list! Whatever your subject specialty it will give you new perspective on your lessons and maybe even get you thinking a little more nerdy." — Carrie Anne Philbin, Director of Education @Raspberry_Pi, Author, @thePSF and @CompAtSch board member, Founder @GeekGurlDiaries, Chair of @CASinclude, Google Certified Innovator

"When teachers ask me how to get started creating a Makerspace, this is the book that I will point them to. What I love is that through his humorous yet personal 'Nerd Alerts' and the embedded reflective 'Maker Thoughts' that help frame thinking at the end of each chapter, readers will not only feel a connection to Mr. Provenzano the teacher but also create a pathway towards authentic Making in the best possible way with their purpose in mind." — Rafranz Davis, Executive Director of Professional and Digital Learning

"Nicholas is a pioneer. His experience, enthusiasm, and good humor make this book a fun and indispensable resource for fostering meaningful Making in your school." — Matt Richardson, Product Evangelist

"The Nerdy Teacher has done with this book what all good Makers and educators do in their classrooms and communities. He took a deep, wonderful topic and made it accessible to everyone by scaffolding the content to offer timely and relevant content to everyone, regardless of experience or prior knowledge. Oh, and the pop culture references and whimsical drawings are awesome, too!" — David Saunders, School Library Maker and DesignSaunders.com

"The best part about *Your Starter Guide to Makerspaces* is the awesome tips? The pop culture references? The stories? It's all of these things, but what makes the book most special is how Nick's voice can be heard throughout it encouraging me to try new things, think big for students, and not to be afraid to step out of my comfort zone. This book is for anyone who's toying with the idea of Makerspaces and hasn't yet taken the plunge. Nick's positive demeanor and warmth shine through every word." — Sherry Gick, Associate Director of Innovative Learning, Five-Star Technology Solutions

"Nick Provenzano writes the perfect book for anyone interested in Making but who doesn't know where to start. *Your Starter Guide to*

Makerspaces lowers the barrier to entry and proves that we are all Makers. The guide is more than a book; it's a companion that new Makers can turn to on their creative journey. We are entering a brave new world in education, and Nick is one of the voices proving that more is possible." — James Sanders, Co-Founder Breakout EDU

"Nick Provenzano has written an awesome guide to 'Making' that not only makes it accessible to everyone but is an awesome and fun read. His mix of personal anecdotes tied into powerful examples of how to get started and move forward *make* this book an awesome addition to a collection for all educators, not just the ones looking to start a 'make space'. Awesome read!" — George Couros, Author of *The Innovator's Mindset* and a global Innovative Teaching, Learning, and Leadership Consultant

YOUR STARTER GUIDE TO MAKERSPACES

By: Nicholas Provenzano
@TheNerdyTeacher

BLEND

This book belongs to

_____

If found, please return to the address of

_____

_____

If you like what you read, send a tweet, post to Instagram, or tell a friend.

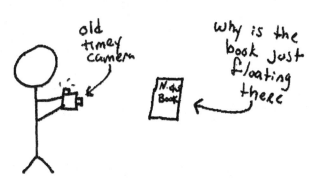

old timey camera

Nick's Book

why is the book just floating there

If you don't like it, I'm truly sorry. Please don't judge.

I Tried! №

ISBN-13: 978-0692786123 (Blend Education)
ISBN-10: 0692786120

Published by Blend

Typesetting: LParnell Book Services

Printed by CreateSpace, An Amazon.com Company

16 17 18 19 20 21 22   7 6 5 4 3 2 1

Contents

*You bought the book and
you want to get Making.
I know the feeling, but I need
you to take the pledge. The
pledge is important. This
is what binds the galaxy
together, what binds you
to the book and the Maker
world. This is legit, so don't
skip it.*

MAKe your own Maker badge!

Looks more like a medal than a badge.

Nerdy MAKing BAdge

The Nerdy Maker Pledge

I (state your name) promise to be the best Maker I can be.

I will not let the eye rolls or the judging eyes scare me
from following my passion.

I will encourage others to do the same,
because Making is a community that accepts everyone.

I will play with gadgets and gizmos and make nerdy references
that make no sense to others and be proud of it.

I will wear my nerdy Making badge proudly on my sleeve
as I strive to change the world for all people.

**I'm a Maker
and I'm proud of it.**

MAKER BOOK

*Didn't that feel great? You're
now ready to dive into this
book and get everything you
need out of Making!*

Introduction

Why Did I Write This Book?

This a great question. I have received many similar questions since I became involved in Making at my school and sharing projects on my site. Here are just a few:

- What is an English teacher doing in a Makerspace?
- Why are you learning how to use a 3D printer?
- Where is the value of coding in the arts?
- What makes you an expert at Making?
- How quickly did the Millennium Falcon make the Kessel Run?

These are all important questions that I will try to explain before you dive further into the text. The most important question is the one I will answer first. *Twelve parsecs. That is how quickly Han made the Kessel Run in the Millennium Falcon.* Now onto the other questions.

"What is an English teacher doing in a Makerspace?"

I have been asked this question more than any other. The idea that a Makerspace is for STEM (Science, Technology, Engineering, and Math) classes is a common misconception. Making does not have a set curriculum. Making can be anything to anyone. I've been a project-based learning (PBL) teacher for a number of years, so using a Makerspace makes complete sense. Later in the book, there will be an entire chapter on PBL that will provide more details on how a Makerspace can make PBL even better. I hope to see students using different tools to demonstrate understanding by having them use the Makerspace in my literature classes.

Nerdy Myths

Myth	Reality
• SAVEd by the Bell: The College Years	• Never happened
• Making is for STEM only	• We are all makers
• The Arts do not belong in makerspaces.	• Makerspace need the Arts to be well rounded.
• Greedo shot first	• It was Han!
• Making is about technology	• Legos, Yarn, Cardboard, Crayons, anything at all can be used to Make.
• Students can't be trusted to create meaningful work.	• Students will make things that are meaningful to them. That's what really matters.
•	•
•	•
•	•
•	•
•	•

Add your myths and realities to the list.

"Why are you learning how to use a 3D printer?" and "Where is the value of coding in the arts?"

I'm learning 3D design because my students will possibly be doing it in class for a project and I want to be able to help them, and because it is very, very cool. It is a tough new skill that I am getting better at, and is very satisfying when you finally print something that you designed from scratch. This process has led me to learn about all the geometry and physics involved in creating objects in 3D. If I want to encourage my students to try new things in class (so I do not get the same poster board or Prezi), I have to demonstrate the possibilities to them by using different tools myself.

The same goes for coding. I was watching students work with Raspberry Pi for their 20% Time project and it blew me away. They were working with Python code and I had no idea what they were doing. They would spend hours in the Makerspace trying to code their Raspberry Pi and I couldn't offer much support. I chose to learn code because I wanted to better support my students.

What I learned was that coding is part of our everyday lives. Yes, code makes the world go round. It's like saying that air is important or that Jabba needs a diet. It's all obvious, but it takes on a different level when you investigate the code. Coding belongs in the arts because it's another language that more and more people will need to learn how to speak. It's the basic foundation for all aspects of computing. Using different design tools and being able to code things to do exactly what you want are great skills for all students. Our job is to prepare them for it now. That is why coding is so valuable to the arts.

"What makes you an expert on Making?"

Nothing. I make stuff and I'm learning to make new stuff. I get my hands dirty and try new things in class with my students. Sometimes these things are awesome, and other times they're big fat failures.

On occasion, they're gigantic failures. Like Kevin Costner in *Waterworld*-type of failure. But that's fine. Making is about failing as much as it's about creating. I'm not claiming to be an expert in Making. I'm a guy who likes to tinker, a guy who built a place at my school to allow students to tinker, and a guy who thinks it's important to get more people Making. And I want to share what I've learned.

What This Book Is and Is Not

This book isn't an analytical approach to Makerspaces with tons of research. It's a book that shares stories about Making and Makerspaces that I've personally experienced. I'm not saying that research or statistics are a bad thing, but that's not what this book is about. In my experience, teachers prefer to hear real cases of teachers doing the work, and that's what I'm sharing here. There are plenty of books that feature super fancy people who have done tons of research to tell you something you already know.

> This book isn't the type of book that tells you everything you're doing is wrong.

This book isn't the type of book that tells you everything you're doing is wrong. This book is accepting of your instructional differences. There are too many books, blogs, tweets, etcetera, out there proclaiming that the new thing is the best thing, and the old thing is terrible, and you're terrible if you're still doing the old thing that used to be the new thing. Ugh.

I love PBL. I think teachers should be using PBL in their class-room. I don't think talking at students all the time is awesome, but I also don't think teachers should toss it. They should do what I'm doing, which is a balance of the two. The same goes for Making and Makerspaces. I'd love to see more teachers involved in Making because I've seen many great things happen with students because of it, but not everyone has to do it all the time. I just want to share something cool that others might want to use.

> **If you see anything that stands out, share it on social media and add #IAmAMaker.**

The rest of the book is filled with the different ways that I approached Making in my school and suggestions on how you can set it up at your school. It also includes well-known and *very* vague popular cultural references that may or may not be funny. I hope this books gets you up and Making in no time at all.

Most importantly, I want you to make this book your own. I want you to annotate it, dog ear the corners, doodle, make lists, cross stuff off, and spill some coffee on it. *If you see anything that stands out, share it on social media and add #IAmAMaker.* At the end of chapters, I'll give you space to share some thoughts for yourself to reflect on, and I want you to write in the book. I'll challenge you to do some things and ask you to be silly. This book is about having fun.

It's *The Nerdy Teacher's Guide*, but I really want you to make it *Your Guide to Makerspaces*. Add all the notes and ideas you want so you can have everything you need when you meet with people and brag about the awesome Makerspace you created at your school. I can't wait to meet you and see the awesome things you have done with this book.

Allons-y!

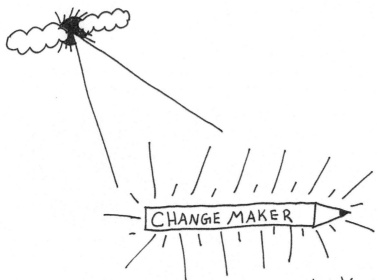

The Most Powerful Maker tool
In the whole wide ~~woold~~ Universe

Find your change MAKER and start
Changing the world!

No Pressure! Start with this book
and go from there.

— Nerdy Maker
Nicholas Provenzano

Maker Thoughts

Write down everything you think you know about
Makerspaces here. When you finish the book,
come back and see if anything has changed.

_____

_____

_____

_____

_____

_____

_____

_____

_____

_____

_____

_____

_____

_____

_____

_____

_____

_____

_____

Nerdy Work

I want you to go to the Internet and find something you would love to Make, but have no idea how to. The crazier, the better. Check out Instructables.com for great projects.

What do you want to Make?

_____

_____

_____

_____

Where did you find it?

_____

_____

_____

_____

Why do you want to Make this?

_____

_____

_____

_____

1

So, What Is Making?

Before we get into how to create a space to Make, we need to define what Making is so we can all be on the same page. Every Maker will have a slightly different definition, but this is the one that I like:

**Making is the creation
of something new
that was not there before.**

Some might suggest that my definition is too broad or vague. I would agree with them. It's broad and a bit vague for a reason. Making should not be constrained by a strict definition. It needs to be huge to let every single person in so we all can Make something awesome. Making is inclusive or, at least, it should be. Making can be the great leveler. Everyone can do it. People can Make with computer code, they can Make with paints and clay, they can Make with yarn, they can Make with Legos, they can Make with pencil and scrap paper, and they can Make with whatever they get their hands on. That is what makes Making so awesome.

Let's get rid of the idea that Making and Makerspaces are for STEM classes or programs only. That's not the case. We need to add the "A" (for arts) to STEM and create STEAM. There is so much the "A" can bring to Makerspaces it's crazy to suggest that the "A" does not belong. The arts bring everything together in STEAM, and it won't be ignored if I have anything to do about it. I'll put it this way: STEM without the "A" is like a DeLorean without a flux capacitor. It's still cool but not as cool.

> We, as individuals, define Maker for ourselves. We determine what a Maker is for us.

Who Is a Maker?

We seem to have the need to define everything we see. Everything needs a label, and there has to be a strict set of guidelines that go with that label if you want to qualify. It makes people feel better about themselves if they know where everything belongs.

Being a Maker does not fit that mold.

We, as individuals, define Maker for ourselves. We determine what a Maker is for us. Maker to you could be knitting quietly on the couch and creating cool winter hats. Maker for someone else could be building the robot (named Kevin) that Screech had on *Saved by the Bell*. A Maker could be someone who dives into 3D design to make special Mr. Belvedere-themed coasters. Having the title of Maker defined by someone else is ridiculous, and it seems to be the antithesis of what being a Maker is all about.

Creating more opportunities for students to Make and celebrate those creations is how we increase the likelihood that these students will continue to be creators and not just consumers.

Any person who wants to create something can do it. That's a very empowering thing to share with students. Everyone has the opportunity to sit and create something brand new. Every child is a Maker. *Creating more opportunities for students to Make and celebrate those creations is how we increase the likelihood that these students will continue to be creators and not just consumers.*

Some people are just born to Make. At least, that's what people will tell you. I believe we are all Makers, but it doesn't hurt to surround children with Makers. As teachers, we need to keep this Maker spirit alive in our students. It's unfair to assume that every student will have a supportive Making environment at home. I was lucky; my Mom and Dad were both Makers.

From the Nerd Files:

When I was growing up, my dad was going through medical school and we lived in the city of Detroit. We didn't have much. We never felt like it, but we realized when we got older the sacrifices our parents made. I have vivid memories of Mom making summer clothes for us, and of my dad doing something in his basement workshop. He was a very handy guy and I always thought that was cool. The one thing that will always remind me about how awesome my parents were to us growing up is He-Man.

In a house of three boys, cartoons ruled the world. That would prove to be a very expensive love for my parents. We loved watching *G.I. Joe*, *Voltron*, *Transformers* and *He-Man*. We had some of the action figures and would stage epic battles for Eternia in our house. When the Castle Grayskull and Snake Mountain playsets were announced, we had to have them. At the time, they seemed so expensive. I recently looked online and saw the price back then was around $25–$30. Today, that doesn't seem like a ton of money, but it was to a family that saved ketchup packets from McDonald's to use at home. ▶

(Nerd Files continued)

We wrote our letters to Santa, and on Christmas we received the best (and coolest) castle and mountain we could have ever hoped for. Our parents made them from wood and painted them for us. My mom stitched together a felt snake to attach to Snake Mountain, and Castle Grayskull had a working drawbridge. There were little shelves on the inside of the castle and mountain so we could stand the characters and play. Those presents will always be the greatest gifts I have ever received.

My parents didn't have much, but they made something for their kids that mattered. That's the beauty of Making. It's creating something you want and sharing it with others. When we got older, we gave the sets to cousins so they could play with them as they grew up. Those handmade presents were a hundred times better than anything Mattel could have put together.

I can look back at that, and the many other experiences I've had with my family, and see what sparked the creative spirit in me. I took things apart because I saw my dad do it. I made things because my parents made things. My dad built a pond when I was younger, so I built a pond when I had my own house. These experiences forged who I am today, and I think it's important to help students have these experiences at school. Especially if they're not getting them at home.

I'm not saying that every student should be a Maker. I'm suggesting that all students should have an opportunity to have those experiences—and that support is available for the ones who want to explore further.

You are a Maker!!

Self Portrait

Thumbs up!

Teacher as Maker

I think most teachers don't view themselves as Makers. Sadly, most teachers view themselves as *just teachers*. I can't stand that, and I even say that about myself sometimes. We are so much more than *just teachers*. We are allies, friends, counselors, therapists, cheerleaders, coaches, and so much more for our students. We are constantly juggling the different things that are going on in our classes every single day. This leads us to forget how tough and meaningful our work is in the classroom. One important hat that we wear is that of the Maker. Every teacher is a Maker.

You might not think of yourself as a Maker, but you are. You make things every single day. You craft lesson plans, build bulletin board displays, create new curriculum, make awards for students, and make so many different things, but you have never really thought about it that way.

Making is very much a way of thinking. Teachers need to accept the fact that they are Makers. That acceptance will help us encourage students to be Makers. As we grow as Makers, we will define what Maker means to each of us as individuals, and we will empower students to become the Makers they want to be.

Nerd Alert

When I think about Making in schools and "Teachers as Makers," I'm reminded of an old *MacGyver* episode. It was called "Hell Week," and was such a cool episode. The focus was a group of students who had to create a barricade room. They needed to create a clever way to keep people out of their dorm room. The goal of the other students was to find a way in. Think of it as a reverse Breakout EDU Room. Here is a clip of the best room from that episode (https://goo.gl/muH2Eo). ▶

(Nerd Alert continued)

Of course, a kid cheats, and the other kid freaks out and threatens to kill himself because he thought his project should have been unbeatable. This really was a side commentary on the dangers of grade obsession. Anyway, as a kid, I thought it was cool to come up with something that would lock people out of a room. The kids seemed so smart, and I remember trying to come up with crazy and complicated ways to lock people out of mine.

That episode really inspired my Making mentality. One memory that stands out is when I locked my brother in a walk-in safe. At one point, I lived in a pretty old house that had this walk-in safe with a huge vault door. The previous owners had converted it into an office. It was pretty cool, but the door wouldn't lock. The combination to the lock had been lost years ago. Well, I didn't let that get in my way.

I was obsessed with trying to find out how I could get the combination to this safe. I started out using all the tried and true methods from TV and movies. I borrowed a stethoscope from my Dad and tried to listen to the lock. I had no idea what I was listening for, but I was supposed to hear something. I tried spinning it around a bunch of times and giving it a tap with a mallet. I'm pretty sure that worked for Yosemite Sam. I'm not sure why it didn't work for me. Finally, I dove into the early Internet and looked up information on safe cracking. I found the answer within a few minutes.

On the inside of the door, there was a set of screws that attached to a backplate. If I unscrewed them, I would be able to view the lock mechanism. The inside of a large combination lock is very cool. You can see the tumblers and the little space that represents each number. It took me a few minutes, but I matched each number with the space on the back with a number on the front. I had hacked the combination to the safe! ▶

(Nerd Alert continued)

The next thing for me to do was lock my brother in the safe. That was the easy part. I lured him in and shut the door. Hey, there was a light in the room, so I'm not a total monster! It was funny and totally worth being grounded for the day. When my dad found out that I was able to get the combination to the safe, he offered a wry smile that showed me he was impressed before issuing the punishment. It was the easiest time I ever served.

I feel like that *MacGyver* episode is a perfect example of complex problem solving and the Maker spirit hard at play, giving students the freedom to approach a broad problem, keeping people out of the room, and letting them use their creative skills to solve it. It has everything you want to see in a lesson designed to test the creative and critical thinking skills of students. I feel this is why we're seeing such an explosion of Breakout EDU in classrooms across the country.

Teachers are flexing their Making skills to come up with impressive lessons that support student creativity and problem solving. The more that our students encounter these types of problem-based lessons, the stronger their skills will become, and they will be able to better handle bigger problems they will face outside of school in future jobs. *As teachers, we need to prepare our students for these inevitable challenges, and Making lessons that support this type of student learning is important for all students.* The teacher as a Maker is important if we want our students to become problem solvers. If the teacher is a Maker and there is a space for students to grow as Makers, then we will

Flex Yours

Making Muscle!!

have a generation of students ready to tackle the tough problems the world will face in the coming years.

Makers Are Storytellers

I've been lucky to be around many great Makers over the past couple of years. They have done some amazing things. I was invited to the White House to kick-off the National Week of Making, and one of the things I heard someone say really resonated with me: Everything that is made has a story.

As an English teacher, this jumped out at me. Yes, everything we make has a story, and we are all storytellers. I have been telling that to students for years. We are designed to be storytellers. Going all the way back to early cave paintings, we have had a compulsion to tell our story. Look around your classroom and see all of the student work you have. I bet that each one of those pieces has a story you could tell anyone who wanted to know. They all have meaning to you and the person who made it. There is value that a casual observer might not see, but there is a story and it's powerful to those involved.

We need to remind our students, and other educators, that we are Makers and Storytellers. Everything we make—whether it is a painting, sculpture, knit hat, or scale replica of the Serenity with a tiny Wash at the helm—has a story, and we need our students to share their story. While we will still consume more than we create, we can do our best to try and balance it.

The most important thing I want you to think about after this chapter is that we are all Makers and our students are natural-born Makers. Makerspaces are a great way to support Makers and come up with some great lessons to support curriculum.

Maker Thoughts

What is your Maker story? What drives you to Make?

_____

_____

_____

_____

_____

_____

_____

_____

_____

_____

_____

_____

_____

_____

_____

_____

_____

_____

_____

Nerdy Work

Sketch out your favorite toys as a child. Draw them as best you can on the page below doing something you had them do as a kid.

2

I Know What Making Is, but Why Should I Care?

You now have an understanding of what Making is, but you might be wondering why you need a Makerspace. This is a common question that needs to be addressed because "why" is probably the first question an administrator will ask if you want to build a Makerspace in your school. Here are some of the reasons Makerspaces can be awesome for the classroom/school as a whole.

Freedom

For most students, their educational journey has been mapped out for them since they started their first day of school. They have little choice once they're entered into a track. Teachers seem to understand the value of choice, but our system doesn't allow for our students to choose much. A Makerspace gives students the opportunity to do what they want, when they want. At the high school level, a Makerspace in the media center is a great way to give students a place to do something they want without interference from the school curriculum. In middle or elementary school, having a space in the classroom or media center where students can be given free time works the same way. We want our students to explore new and exciting things they are passionate about on their own terms. I know that sounds crazy for our educational system, but crazy ideas seem to have a way of making the most change. The new freedom students have found in the Makerspace can support other important aspects of a Makerspace.

From the Nerd Files:

One day, I headed to the Makerspace to see if any students needed support. As I scanned the busy space, I noticed one of my students sitting on the ground against the wall. She was working with a student I didn't recognize and they were sketching things on a piece of paper and looking at their phones. The students had a rough diagram of a horse leg and hoof with lots of arrows and scribbles. When I asked the students what they were doing, they told me they were working to design a prosthetic hoof for horses who have a break so they don't have to be put down.

I was blown away.

These students were spending their free time designing and trying to create a 3D printed hoof to help horses. The crazy part is that neither of them ride or work with horses. They just thought it would be a nice thing to create. That is the creativity I love to see from our students, and I was very lucky to see these two creating something in our Makerspace.

This is a perfect example of what can happen when you give students a free space to meet and collaborate. They found something they both thought was interesting and worked on it. They brought their lunches and designed while sitting on the ground. It was such a laid-back approach to something so helpful. That is what time and space can bring to the educational world, and that is a great reason why Makerspaces are important to schools.

Creativity

Creativity is one of the first things cut from schools and classrooms when budgets are slashed. The arts are consistently destroyed by budget cuts and it is next to impossible to make up for the void that is left behind. Curriculum changes are forcing more textbook use, and a focus on specific skills is forcing many teachers to stop fun and interesting projects to cover cookie-cutter curriculum. It's a shame and it needs to change.

Makerspaces are a great way to bring back creativity and support deeper learning. Some of the best projects I've seen at school have come out of the Makerspaces. Students are given an opportunity to explore ideas that are interesting to them, and they can do it with the tools they need at their disposal. When I write about designing a Makerspace and outfitting it with tools, you will see how this can impact the types of things students can do. No matter what they choose, students will love having a place for creativity. That is what Makerspaces are all about, fostering the creative spirit in people.

Innovation

Creativity can be linked to innovation, but they don't always go hand in hand. You can be creative in making a very cool Sarlacc cosplay costume and the Great Pit of Carkoon, but it might not be innovative. Innovation can take place anywhere, but having a dedicated spot that encourages and supports innovative ideas and people can lead to extraordinary projects.

Students love the opportunity to try to solve problems in new ways. These challenges can be teacher created or student generated. You can even open the newspaper and try to find problems that students can work on and solve. There are many possibilities for innovation once students are given a space that allows them to be innovative.

However, there is more to innovation than giving students a space. With access to the Makerspace, teachers will and should become more innovative as well. Lessons will take on new life as a new space with new tools becomes available to the teacher and the students. Standard class projects could change into dynamic 3D-designed projects. Students design and print their ideas, and use a green screen to create a commercial to sell their product. Knowing there are more options to create can help teachers and students innovate their lessons and projects. You cannot make students be innovative, but you can allow them access to the tools and the space to become innovative when the mood strikes.

From the Nerd Files:

I had assigned an independent project for my students one semester. I tasked them with identifying one problem and its solution. Those were the basic guidelines. I was blown away by the different projects the students created. Some dealt with trying to clean up oceans, and others included ways to improve Wi-Fi in the home. Two students identified a school problem that could change the way students go to the bathroom. ▶

(Nerd Files continued)

The group wanted to create an easier way for students to sign in and out of the classroom to go to the bathroom. The school recently required students to sign out on a sheet of paper and sign back in while recording the time. The students found this tedious and disruptive to the class. They took a Raspberry Pi and started to work on a way to connect a scanner to it so students would just scan their IDs and would log the info and time stamp into a Google sheet. Then teachers or admins could access if needed.

I watched as the students struggled to get things to work for them. They coded something incorrectly and got frustrated when the OS didn't load on the Raspberry Pi. As a teacher, it was tough for me to do, but they were learning so much along the way, I didn't want to interfere. When the semester was near its end, the two students had a chance to present their project to a group of superintendents from the Metro Detroit area. The room was filled with nodding heads and impressed smiles. Our superintendent even told the students he would love to see a pilot of their invention in our schools and offered the full support of the district to make it happen! The kids altered their schedule and set up an independent study so they could continue their work on their project in the Makerspace while they were at school.

As of this writing, the students are in the beta phase of their project and they are close to piloting it in a classroom (mine). Watching them go through their trials and errors as they tried to create something brand new has been inspiring. They have shown me how Makerspaces can lead to wonderful innovations.

Innovation isn't something you can force on people, especially students. Innovation tends to come from a need and the space and freedom to explore. Their innovations will happen organically, and students will learn amazing new things on their own.

Equity

I have always felt that school should be a great equalizer. Students should have access to the best education no matter where they live. Sadly, where you are born has everything to do with the type of education you will receive. I have been very lucky to teach in a district where the majority of our students have access to some of the best resources in the state. Other schools do not have the resources to create a Makerspace. This is especially true if Makerspaces are all about shiny and expensive gadgets.

This book will cover some of those shiny gadgets, but Makerspaces are more than that. Making is a way of thinking. A spirit that is larger than any gadget that can be brought into a room. Handing students paper and crayons can lead to amazing creations in a Makerspace. While funding equality seems to be many years away, opportunity to Make can be brought to every student in the country. As teachers, we find the time, space, and resources for the things that matter most for our students. Makerspaces matter, and it's possible to create them for all students so they can have the same Making experiences no matter where they are.

Collaboration

Properly designed Makerspaces support and encourage collaboration. There will always be a time and a place for people to fly solo on different projects. You do not want to take that away from students. However, collaboration is an important skill, and we want to encourage students to embrace working with others with the understanding that different people bring various skills to the table. These skills can help solve bigger problems and potentially forge unlikely friendships.

Nerd Alert

There are so many rag-tag stories I could reference when it comes to the value of collaboration, but one of my favorite examples would be the cult classic *Monster Squad*. In this amazing movie, a group of kids (who are from all different backgrounds) come together because they love all things related to monsters. They love monster movies and comics. They meet in the lead character's tree house to discuss monster-related items. Not surprisingly, monsters happen to come to town, and these kids need to come together and save their community and the earth from Dracula and his evil minions.

The music montage is an excellent scene because it shows the kids working together to prepare for their fight with pure evil. They are making weapons by melting silver taken from their parents' houses and sharpening spikes in a woodshop. These kids needed to solve a "real-life" problem and did so by Making. Instead of using the cramped tree house, the kids would have been better off having a space in their school to meet and share these common passions for monsters and monster defense. If not for their Maker attitude, the world would be overrun with monsters.

NERD!

Monster Squad

Spoiler Alert!

Ahhh

Woo Hoo

There is a myth that students do not want to work together. They just want to sit by themselves and play video games. People who don't play video games say these things. Video games have become more collaborative than ever. Teams from all over the world form to battle all types of monsters and terrorist organizations, which requires tons of planning, organization, and communication. Over and over again we see how students want to collaborate in their daily lives, but most schools aren't giving them enough opportunities to do it.

Fun

I honestly believe this has become a forbidden "F" word in education. When did having fun and learning become mutually exclusive concepts? Not everything is going to be fun, but we can try to make learning and exploring new things a fun experience.

How can a Makerspace make learning fun? Great question! Having a space does not make learning more fun. It sounds like everything would be better by saying you have one, but you need to use it properly to get the most out of it. It would be like you have a real lightsaber. That would be awesome. However, not using it correctly or letting it sit and gather dust would be a complete waste of a perfectly good lightsaber. You will never become a Jedi if you stare at the lightsaber and carry a shriveled green guy on your back all the time. You need to use it to make it work for the best.

A Makerspace can be a free spot for students to drop in and do some work, but it can also be a tool to support student learning in fun and exciting ways. If your Makerspace has a green screen, have students film their own PSAs (public service announcements) or book trailers. Engage students in the design process as they learn to write "How-To" assignments and practice their writing skills.

The best thing about a Makerspace is that it can support whatever a student or teacher needs if they have the will to make it happen. The fun comes along because students are involved in engaging content that appeals to them. We need to remember that having fun in the classroom is OK, and that sometimes, the noisiest and messiest classes learn the most.

> A Makerspace can be a free spot
> for students to drop in and do some work,
> but it can also be a tool to support
> student learning in fun and exciting ways.

No Silver Bullet

A Makerspace is not a silver bullet that is going to destroy the ills that menace education. Too many people tout their new thing as the key to changing education for everyone and solving all of our problems. I challenge anyone to show how their "thing" has solved all the problems in education. Makerspaces are another tool that allows students and teachers to explore teaching and learning in a different way.

The following chapters are going to explore the different ways Making and Makerspaces can impact learning and teaching. Some of them will apply to what you're doing in the classroom, and others might be far from where you are currently. My goal is to show all of the different possibilities for all the types of teachers and learners. Like all books, take what works for you and identify areas you want to focus on in the coming school year.

Maker Thoughts

How would you use a Makerspace in your
school or classroom? Let your imagination
run wild here.

_____

_____

_____

_____

_____

_____

_____

_____

_____

_____

_____

_____

_____

_____

_____

_____

Nerdy Work

Plan out a lesson that requires you to be in a Makerspace to complete. Plan it from start to finish. This will be your first Makerspace lesson ever!

Thoughts & IDEAS on MAKING

EXTRA NOTES

_____

_____

_____

_____

_____

_____

_____

_____

_____

_____

_____

_____

_____

_____

_____

_____

_____

_____

_____

_____

_____

_____

3

Where Does a Makerspace Go in a School?

The easiest answer is anywhere you want, but you probably are looking for a bit more guidance. There are many options on where to place a Makerspace, but it really depends on what your goals are for the space.

Bad Ideas

The one thing that you want to avoid is the closed off Makerspace. This is a space in a room that students don't have regular access to throughout the day. The impulse to place it in a room that is under lock and key because of the expensive equipment is natural, but that defeats the purpose of a Makerspace. Makerspaces should be in public spaces that students have access to whenever they want.

Avoid placing the Makerspace in a room that will have regular classes. Having a Maker class that meets in the Makerspace could be awesome and a great goal to shoot for down the line, but if that class prevents the walk-in from Making, then the Makerspace is just a classroom used for a specific purpose. You want students to come and go throughout the day. Teachers can also schedule time in the space to send students to work on projects. That would not be possible if a class meets there every day.

If students want to go to the Makerspace and create amazing things, they should not need to jump through a bunch of hoops to get there. To get the Holy Grail in *Indiana Jones and the Last Crusade*, Indy needed to traverse some pretty complicated obstacles. Students should have an easier time finding and accessing the Makerspace in your school. Avoid complex signup sheets or reservation calendars. You want a student or a teacher to walk in and get to work.

We tend to want to plan and organize every aspect of our spaces, but this is the space where we want students to freely come and go as ideas come to them. Too many procedures will limit the number of students who will use the space.

From the Nerd Files:

When it comes to spaces for children to learn, we don't need to look much further than our own homes. We didn't have much growing up, but we did have a space in the basement that was ours to play (and it held many of our toys). We could go down and come up with all of the crazy adventures of He-Man and G.I. Joe to take as they fight the giant monster Teddy Ruxpin. It was the go-to space in the house for the brothers to play. We used this space when we would play Dungeons and Dragons, and this was also the space where we would create our blanket/pillow forts. *It was our space and we knew it.* These spaces allowed us to have access to everything we needed to create the amazing stories that would entertain us for hours. ▶

(Nerd Files continued)

I've created a similar space in my house for my son. I did it without thinking about it. It was an organic creation. We wanted to have a space for his toys that would not clutter the house and would allow him to go and play when he wanted. We decided on the space that he would frequently bring his toys to play. We built our space around him. He loves to play with his cars and characters. He has his Kylo Ren matchbox car fighting against his Ninja Turtles as they race around the room avoiding the Sphero BB-8 I control. I am amazed at the wonderful and creative ideas he comes up with in his space, and I hope he has the chance to find a space in school that is equally supportive of his creative spirit.

Good Ideas

The Classroom (Best for Elementary):

I know I wrote that putting a Makerspace in a classroom under lock and key or with classes all of the time is a bad idea, but this is different. Elementary classes are their own little ecosystem of learning. Most teachers have the students all day or most of the day. They need to teach the majority of subjects while in their classroom. Mini-Makerspaces are perfect for the elementary classroom. I wrote that a Makerspace needs to be a place that is easy to access, and the room where they spend most of their time is the best place for that age.

A Mini-Makerspace in the classroom should have its own little spot. It should be clearly identified and students should be able to use it during the day for various assignments or free time. Add some comfy chairs and little storage units to keep their projects. Really make the space inviting to all students.

Mini Makerspace

Media Center (Best for All Levels)

This is the best place for a Makerspace for so many different reasons. The media center, or library, has always been the hub for learning in a school. If it isn't, a Makerspace is a great way to recenter it. We want students to have access and be in a comfortable and safe place to try new things, and the media center is a great place to start. Here are the big reasons to place a Makerspace in the media center:

■ *Space.* Media centers tend to have the most open space. There tends to be unused reference sections that can be converted into Makerspaces now that so much research takes place online. You want a space that is flexible, and media centers are usually designed to allow for the movement of tables and chairs. An open space where everything can be seen is a perfect spot for a Makerspace.

■ *Furniture.* Media centers will already have tables and chairs that can be used for Makerspaces. This saves on a huge expense down the line. Comfy chairs and couches are an excellent addition to any Makerspace. We want students to be comfortable while they research and Make. Finding some nice furniture for cheap can add a level of comfort that students will enjoy.

■ *Supervision.* Makerspaces will need to have a set of eyes on them to check in on the students. The media center is already staffed by a librarian or other aides and they can help monitor and support students in the Makerspace (more on this later).

■ *Access.* Media centers are open all day, and often before/after school. This gives students many opportunities throughout the day to access the space and get creative. The more access students have to something, the more likely they are to utilize it. More access also equals higher engagement.

Another part of access is for the teachers. We want teachers to use the space and see what it can do for them and for their students. If teachers have an easy time getting to the space and using it to create lessons, there will be more students using the space for projects, which will increase the use of the space outside of their classes and create more Makers. It's a win all around!

Nerd Alert

I love big, open, and collaborative spaces. There is an awesome energy in those rooms. They make me think about *Star Trek: The Next Generation* and Ten Forward. Ten Forward was the social hub of the Enterprise. People would show up, share stories, play games, and just connect. They would sometimes get amazing advice from the bartender and go and save the day.

Guinan, played wonderfully by Whoopi Goldberg, was always there to offer sage advice and support the members of the Enterprise. This is exactly what teachers should be doing in the Makerspace with students. The students should arrive and get support, but not have their problems solved for them. The power of Guinan was that she could steer people in the right direction by asking the right questions and being there to listen. As a teacher, I have found it to be the most effective way to support many of my students. A Makerspace in the library/media center is the perfect spot to connect and collaborate with students and provide the guidance they need.

There are other solid reasons to place a Makerspace in a library/media center, but those four stand out as the best to start your conversation. Moving forward with this idea will require you get some allies. Putting a Makerspace in a public spot in the school is going to take some time, effort, pleading, bargaining, and more to make it happen.

Maker Thoughts

List all of the needed furniture and other space
requirements you want in your Makerspace.
Tables, chairs, lockers, hammocks, hover-
boards, etcetera.

Nerdy Work

Design what you want your space to look like. Draw the Makerspace as you see it in your brain. Be as detailed as you can. Go for it!

E
X
T
R
A

N
O
T
E
S

4

Making Allies

There are going to be people who do not get the whole "Making" thing. The idea of giving up space to students so they can create new things could be a very foreign concept for some educators stuck in a "test, test, test" school culture. The best suggestion would be to have them buy this book because of how awesome it is ☺! If budgets are tight, you could just find different ways to sway them to your team. There are various groups of people who are worth forming *Survivor*-esque alliances with to ensure a Makerspace will grow in your school.

Warning: Every school has a different dynamic when it comes to administration. It's important to think about how your dynamic works before trying to form alliances. You don't want to accidentally step on any toes as you try to bring everyone together or you might have a Red Wedding-type event in the future. Well, it might not be that bad, but you might not end up with a Makerspace and that would be sad.

Teachers and Teacher Librarians

Teachers and teacher librarians are keys to forming the ultimate Making alliance. Without them, everything else will fall apart. Both groups hold powerful positions when it comes to putting together an alliance.

Teachers

For teachers, they will be able to support the use of the space over the course of the school year. Connect with them and find out the different lessons they use and the students who could benefit from a space. They're the eyes and ears for a Makerspace. They're also the mouth. They can help promote it to students, parents and administrators. A Makerspace needs to be designed for everyone. If teachers feel like they can bring their students down to use the space or encourage their students to use it for project work, the space can grow and gain significant traction.

Sell teachers on the wide variety of creative work students will be able to do in a Makerspace for class projects. Tell them about the innovative projects students could do with a green screen. Engage in discussions around how a large collaborative space might spark some creative ideas for their lesson plans. Teachers need to see this new space as a valuable asset for their work or they will not be supportive. If you can show them the power of the space beforehand, they will be more likely to get on board with what you are hoping to create. Sometimes just showing them how you would use the space is enough to get others to support the idea of Makerspace.

Teacher Librarians

Teacher librarians (TLs) are also essential in setting up a Makerspace and creating a culture of Making. The best space for a Makerspace is in the library/media center. If you want to set up a Makerspace and you've consulted with everyone else before talking to them, you will have a Nightvale-Level Librarian Rage sent

Teacher Librarians

your way. We are all very protective of our spaces and TLs are no different. I have been very lucky that my TL has been a strong partner in the creation of our Makerspace. We worked together to design the place and fill it with goodies. I can trust her to manage the space when I'm not there and be an advocate for it to others in the building.

The benefit for the TL is that it will drive more traffic to the library/media center and it will become a larger hub for learning. The increase in students offers TLs a chance to try new things and get creative with their own programming. By centering a Makerspace in the library, it brings more attention to the space, and that is always a bonus for creative learning. This evolution of a library/media center into a full learning center with a Makerspace can be a powerful change in education, and TLs have a chance to help lead that change.

Form your teacher librarian alliance as soon as you can or your Makerspace might crash and burn.

Administrators

You have the TL and other teachers signed up, and it's now time to take on the Iron Throne! I mean, talk to the administration. Every administrator is different. It's important to have a good idea of how much your principal likes to be looped into things. Some want to know every detail and be involved from the start, and others might not want to hear anything until you have a final proposal in hand. Here is one thing that can work to get the building administration on board with a Makerspace:

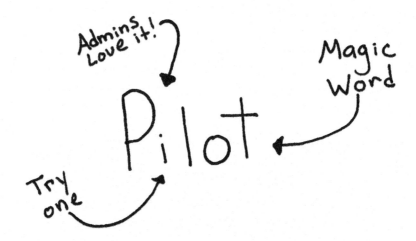

Call it a pilot. Pilot programs are one of the favorite things for an administrator to hear and brag about to others. Pilots have the potential of failure built into them, so they are risk-free ventures. Telling your administrator that you have teachers and other staff ready to try a pilot program where students would work with tools to enhance STEAM skills is a wonderful way to get them excited. Pilots allow the teacher to take risks and try things without the fear of repercussions. That freedom can lead to some amazing creations and concepts in the space that will support student learning. For admins, they will get to brag about the innovative pilot program their teachers put together to support student STEAM skills. If you're not a fan of the word *pilot*, go for the word *beta*. That's a very fancy techy sounding word that people also like to say.

Working with administrators will be key as the Makerspace takes shape and you start to think about budgets. Dedicating a small startup budget for the Makerspace would be great, and administrators are key in making that happen. It's common to start a pilot with some seed money. Administration can help get money from the district or sign off on any grant requests. They hold the purse strings, so make sure they know what is going on so you can make the Makerspace a reality for your school.

Students

Let's face it; students outnumber us by a large margin in schools. Individually, they're small and easy to control like a tribble on the USS Enterprise. As a group, they are an unstoppable force like Nic Cage in every Nic Cage movie ever. The key is to get students excited about the idea of a Makerspace. They can be one of the strongest allies and will help you get the other groups in line.

Giving students the Making bug is a great way to win them over. Holding special events after school for students interested in Making is a great way to spark their interest. You can have fun competitions that involve simple items. These could be paper airplane competitions, design contests, coding hack-a-thons, and anything else that is easy to set up and allows the students to explore. Passionate students will be drawn to it like Luke to Blue Milk. By creating these opportunities for students to Make, you will also be able to gauge their interests and find more ways to support them.

Once the students are hooked, they will ask for more events and how they can do creative work after school. This can start the momentum to putting in a larger space that is stocked with a diverse set of "Maker-goodies" based on student interest. You really want the students to drive the growth of the space. It's great to have passionate teachers who want to build a Makerspace, but nothing beats student passion. Having the right people see excited students Making and tinkering is the best way to sell any idea.

With the students firmly by your side, it's time to look for the next set of allies in building your space.

Parents

Parents are awesome. They can help make any project a reality with the right motivation. With the students firmly entrenched in Making, the parents will not be far behind. They will be interested in what their children are doing, and some will be interested in the different ways they can support them. Some of my most successful initiatives were with the support of parents. They can help organize events or provide supplies. They use their own parenting network to get the word out to bring more students into the Makerspace, and then their parents will be involved as well. Parent involvement takes any project to the next level. Sometimes, parents want to help but do not know where they're needed. Reaching out to parents can bring in all the support you need.

Another helpful aspect in forming the alliance with parents is that they might be connected to local businesses. This is huge for a Makerspace! As a teacher, the number of connections you might have that can help a Makerspace could be limited, but that isn't true of parents. The more parents you have, the more possible connections there could be. You want to encourage all parents to help and participate in any way they can. They might be that parent who knows a guy who knows a guy.

Businesses

Businesses have money. I know, spoilers! Many businesses are always looking for ways to support community schools. Sometimes it's by allowing schools to host fundraisers with them, and other times it's a straight donation. The problem that some businesses have is that they sometimes don't know where to spend the money. That is where your huge alliance comes in. Think of your alliance as five mini-robot lions that join forces to create one big robot that can vanquish your enemies. In this case, the large robot will put together a nice presentation to convince business leaders to support a Makerspace instead of using the blazing sword to cut a ro-beast in half.

One of the biggest fears that businesses have when it comes to donating is that they don't know exactly where the money is going to be spent. For a Makerspace, you can show them that their donations purchase something very specific for the space. It could be computers or tablets. It could be crafting supplies or pieces of technology. Heck, it could be knitting yarn. The point is, a specific item to donate toward is more appealing than just dumping money into a school and hoping it goes to something helpful. Making specific requests of businesses is a great way to show them how their donations can directly impact the students. Having the students do the presentation is even better.

Nerd Alert

Whenever I think of individuals coming together, I think of Voltron. I know that some people might think of the Power Rangers, but those guys were lame. The original *Voltron: Defender of the Universe* was peak 80s cartoon watching for me. For those who do not know much about Voltron, it was a cartoon that featured five space explorers (Sven would later be replaced by Princess Allura) who come together to protect the planet Arus and the galaxy from the evil ro-beasts sent by the Witch Haggar at the behest of Prince Lotor and King Zarkon by using the five ancient lion robots that come together to form Voltron. It is amazing.

The premise of most episodes is very similar. One of the characters has an issue, and they believe that they can solve it on their own. While trying to solve the problem, a bad guy shows up and kicks their butt. There is a realization that they need the strength of their combined forces to defeat this monster. They join together and use their blazing sword to kill the monster in one slash. The character thanks all of the friends and tells them that they have learned a valuable lesson. Until the next week rolls along and it happens all over again. ▶

Great for
Slashing
red tape

(Nerd Alert continued)

This entire series is a perfect metaphor for working together with the different stakeholders to create a Makerspace. It might be possible for one or two of the lions to defeat a ro-beast, but it could end badly for everyone. A couple of people might be able to create a Makerspace on their own, but it's difficult. It's all about being open to asking for help and combining your strengths to accomplish great things. The Voltron Force has the same goal, keeping the galaxy safe, and stakeholders in your school have the same goal, supporting learning. By combining forces, the school can be changed in such wonderful ways, and creating Makerspaces is just one of them. I encourage all of you to find your lion and get out there with the support of others and save your school.

Building a Makerspace is a task that requires the skills of many different people. As teachers, we often have to go it alone because that is how our job is set up at times. That approach will cause you plenty of headaches if you try to put together a Makerspace. Gather your team and create the best Makerspace ever.

Maker Thoughts

Write down all the obstacles you expect to face when trying to create a Makerspace at your school. Don't have any? Well, isn't that nice. How about you draw a unicorn instead? Here's a riddle for you: What do a unicorn and a problem-free school initiative have in common? Neither are real! Lolz.

_____

_____

_____

_____

_____

_____

_____

_____

_____

_____

_____

_____

_____

_____

_____

_____

_____

_____

_____

_____

_____

_____

_____

_____

_____

_____

_____

Nerdy Work

Assemble your team here! Who are
your go-to teammates in building
the most amazing Makerspace
your school has ever seen?

5

What Goes in a Makerspace?

Now that you have a space and allies to help put it together, it's time to fill it with awesome equipment that the students will use. This is right and wrong. You're going to want to place things in the Makerspace that you think all Makerspaces should have because you have seen Makerspaces with these things, and you have heard other Makers talk about the very cool equipment they have in their Makerspaces and you want the same cool stuff. *Makerspace envy is a real problem, but it can be overcome with some level-headed thinking and deep breathing.*

I have shared starter kits for Makerspaces in various articles on my site and other places because there is a belief that Makerspaces require certain things. There is some truth to that, but it depends on your school and how invested the students are at the start of the Makerspace process. For me, our students were ready to sit and Make. Also, getting teenagers excited about anything is about as difficult as creating a Patronus Charm as a first-year student at Hogwarts. Am I right?

> Makerspace envy is a real problem, but it can be overcome with some level-headed thinking and deep breathing.

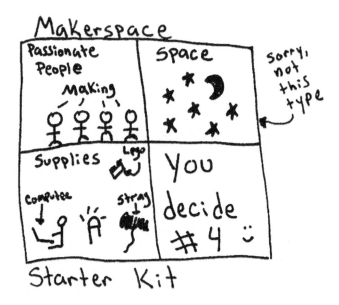

I needed to seed the space with some cool tools to get the students interested in the space. I let them take the space in the direction they wanted. It's a work in progress, but more and more students are using the space for projects and are designing and creating every day.

For those who have a rabid student body ready to get Making, asking them what they want to do is the best way to find out what you need in your Makerspace. If the students really want to design in 3D, some Chromebooks or laptops with access to design software and a 3D printer would be a perfect choice for the space. If the students want to construct buildings, maybe Legos are the way to go. If they are video happy, a green screen could be a perfect addition. Having students involved in the process gives them a sense of ownership that will lead to higher student engagement.

For those who are starting from scratch like I did, here are some cool ideas for what you can have in your Makerspace that might spark the creative elements in your students.

Computers

Stakeholders need to make a decision early on about the type of access the students will have in the Makerspace. Will they be bringing their own devices? If not, what devices will be provided for them? We decided on Chromebooks for our space because we wanted to keep our programs web-based so students could work on these at home. If you have specific programs that students will be using that are not web-based, you will need to consider laptops. The reason I suggest laptops is because you want students to be mobile in a Makerspace. They will need to bounce to different stations to do different things or collaborate with different groups. This freedom to move around is destroyed if the Makerspace is filled with hardwired computers. It just becomes another computer lab if they are stuck at computer stations.

We do have a few set devices that we use for heavy computing. We have a couple of Macs and PCs for video editing, 3D printing, and other larger projects that students might need to work on that a Chromebook will not support. We have not had any issues regarding the use of these devices and everyone seems to respect the work others are doing and don't hog the devices. We have found it to be a nice balance of devices in the space.

We also allow students to bring their own devices and connect to the school Wi-Fi. That is a district policy that has helped keep other devices open for those who don't have their own to bring to school. It has helped prevent the digital divide that could have formed in the Makerspace. A Makerspace without open Wi-Fi is like The Doctor without his sonic screwdriver. It's still pretty amazing but more amazing with it.

From the Nerd Files:

During one class period, I was having students work on a coding unit for the Hour of Code. Students were using the Chromebooks to go over the Hour of Code on their own, but they would pick up the Chromebook to move to other areas in the Makerspace to get help from others when they were stuck. It was nice to see the space being used exactly as it was intended—a collaborative setup that allowed students to move freely from one spot to the other. The students moved easily and naturally and helped one another to accomplish the tasks. At times, students would even use their own devices along with their Chromebooks to get more support for the lessons or even do more research on ideas that popped into their heads while they worked. It was a natural work-flow for students, and this is key when students are trying new things and being creative.

3D Printers

You might want to have students use 3D printers in your Makerspace because you have seen them before and think they are very cool. Let me set the record straight: 3D printers are really freaking cool. They're simply magic. I'm sure there is a bunch of science-y things and engineering things going on, but it's pure magic to watch a piece of jewelry printed right in front of your eyes. It's like watching something appear on the holodeck or repli-cator on *Star Trek: The Next Generation.* I never thought it would be something I would see as commonplace, but they are, and your school can have one. However, there is much more to a 3D printer than printing random stuff.

The real power of 3D printing isn't in the printer; it's in the design process. If you painted an awesome portrait and then placed it on a copy machine to make a copy, you didn't learn anything from the copy; you learned while creating the original product. The same is true for 3D design and printing. The hours of hard work that can go into an original design teach a user so much about geometry and physics. Learning to create something from scratch that adheres to basic design principles discovered on their own is a great learning tool. I've watched students struggle with creating the correct size and shape of objects so they would not topple over on the print bed. I've seen students struggle with their print job because they were designing in millimeters instead of inches. Students achieved a great understanding of these items through the design process, not the printing process. That is the true power of 3D printers. It gives students another tool to learn new and valuable skills.

Code

Code is not a physical tool you can hold and place in a Makerspace, but there are plenty of great devices (Raspberry Pi, Arduino, etc.) that can be best utilized by learning how to code. Computer code is not a new thing. It has been around since we've had computers, but the expansion of Internet-based tools and the accessibility of other tools has made it possible for more schools to create coding programs to support a growing need for coders.

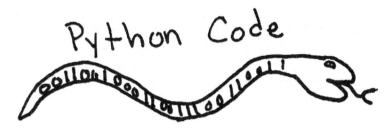

More students are coding than ever before. They're starting at a younger age and becoming more proficient. It really is learning another language. I'm new to the coding world, but I've learned so much from watching students and playing with code myself. The beauty behind coding is that it is not about teaching every single student to become a computer programmer. It's about giving students experience in a tool that is increasingly taking over every aspect of our lives. That sounds scary, and it might be just a few years before Skynet takes over and Arnold is appearing naked at a construction site in California, but until that time, we need to provide students access to coding.

For myself, I have learned how code works, and how it makes other things work. I've written my own lines of code and I have made lights blink faster and then I made them blink slower. I figured out how to make a Raspberry Pi send a text message if a circuit is closed! I have no idea why I would need such a thing, but I now understand the process that makes it possible, and I can apply those concepts to other problems. I'm watching students do it all the time. They're working on different pieces of code and come across other ways their creation could be used.

From the Nerd Files:

We held a Raspberry Pi competition at my school. We gave students a Raspberry Pi kit and told them they could not spend more than $75 on their project. They needed to identify a problem and come up with a solution. Those were the simple instructions, and we were blown away by what the different groups created. ▶

(Nerd Files continued)

One group created an app-based solution that would allow a user to turn their lights on and off. They felt that people in wheelchairs might not be able to reach lights in older houses, so they figured out how to wire the Raspberry Pi to regulate the power on the room lights and control them through a web-based app. It was such a cool idea, but what was even cooler were the different ideas other students came up with during the presentations. It was a full brainstorming session on the different applications for their project. They ranged from starting the coffee maker when you rolled out of bed to powering on and off entire rooms. Now that the kids have an understanding of what they created, they can apply it to other projects however they want. They taught themselves how to do all of the coding. That knowledge is going to serve them well down the line.

The best part of that story is that the students taught themselves to code. I gave them a broad topic and they learned the code they needed to complete their project. I will have more on this in the PBL chapter, but this is a good example of what is possible when students are given an opportunity to explore learning on their own and given access to the tools that allow them to try new things. Makerspaces are designed to give people the chance to create, and coding is the perfect tool to help accomplish that.

Gadgets

It's a lot of fun to play with gadgets and learn about creating by playing with them. We all learn through play. It's the most basic learning strategy that we have been engaging in since birth. Give humans something fun and we will learn everything we can about it. Filling a Makerspace with fun gadgets that encourage play and will require some amount of learning is a great way to engage students in learning. These are just a few gadgets students and I have used in the Makerspace.

SAM Labs

SAM Labs have created a very cool system that allows users to connect their pieces to their computer, phone, or iPad via Bluetooth and have them do almost whatever you want. You can have them read Twitter in search of a specific hashtag and have a light blink every time the hashtag is used. You can then set it up to auto-tweet in response to those tweets. There is so much more you can do, and students have had so much fun playing with them.

3Doodler Pen

3D design can be done with a pen! That sounds like something super crazy and reminds me of that scene from the *Supergirl* movie. Back on Krypton, Kara draws a flying bug or something and it comes to life. That's like a 3D pen. The 3Doodler allows you to draw in 3D on the spot. You can choose from different colors and different filaments. It's very handy and safe to use for kids. This is nice and fun addition to a Makerspace.

littleBits

I love littleBits. Each bit is part of a circuit that you can build to accomplish something. Some activate a fan and others provide the temperature. The bits snap together with magnets and do not require any soldering or coding. I gave a set to my son and he created a push-button flashlight. He put three bits together and he was all set. He turned to me and said he could now find all of the things he lost under the couch. It's a simple and fun way to get started with Making.

Makey Makey

Have you ever wanted to play digital bongos with a banana? Of course you have, and Makey Makey now lets you do that. With some jumper wires and one board, you can connect a directional pad and buttons to other objects and interact with your computer. I've seen students use Play-Doh, oranges, raspberries, pennies, and anything that is conductive to create gamepads. While these might not be practical uses of the wires, they teach the concepts of how wires can be used and how input and output work. Watching kids of all ages play with this is so much fun.

Raspberry Pi

Raspberry Pi is a $35 computer! Yes, you read that correctly. This computer is the size of a credit card that runs a full operating system. You connect to an HDMI monitor, add a keyboard and mouse, and you're ready to go. I became a Raspberry Pi Certified Educator and I keep learning all of the cool things that can be done with Pi. You can run Scratch, you can play *Minecraft*, and you can program the Pi to do just about anything! Check out RaspberryPi.org for tons of resources on using Pi in the classroom.

Kano

This is a computer that students build on their own. A complete kit comes with a Raspberry Pi, screen, keyboard, and all of the plugs needed to make it work. The directions teach you how to assemble it, and it walks you through setting up the software. From there, students can create their own snake game, pong game, and play *Minecraft*! They can log in and earn badges for the various accomplishments. It's a great way to gamify coding and creation using computing skills.

EZ-Robot

The dream of every nerd is to build their own robot. We all want to have the personal robot butler to do our bidding. It's now easier than ever to build your own robot and have it do what you want. EZ-Robot is a great system for a user to assemble a robot, program it, and watch it go. You can have it dance to music, react to specific voice commands, respond to objects or colors, and so much more. The computer interface is amazing, and I've watched students practice their coding and critical-thinking skills as they programmed their robots to navigate obstacle courses in the Makerspace. Students gain serious programming skills while working on these robots and that is a huge plus to have in any Makerspace.

Nerd Alert

When you talk about gadgets, you have to think about Batman. He had a gadget for everything. He even had shark repellent when he was attacked by a shark! It might seem like Batman has all of these gadgets because he thinks so far ahead, but he has these gadgets because he needed them at one point and didn't have them. He then created them in case the need would arise again. Filling a Makerspace works under the same premise. You don't fill it with anything and everything you can think of because the thing you might need most might not be there and you no longer have the resources to get exactly what you need. Fill your space with the gadgets you need ■ based on demand. ▶

(Nerd Alert continued)

Batman also had some gadgets he knew he would use on a regular basis. He had his batarang, smoke pellets, grappling hook, and a few others. These were his go-to items when things got crazy. For a Makerspace, the same concept applies. There will be some things that you will absolutely need on a regular basis. These will be computers and various programs. You will know what you need based on your experience. There is nothing worse than wasting resources on things that go unused. We have seen districts do it and we do not want to repeat those mistakes.

Ultimately, what I'm trying to say is that you're basically Batman because you chose to place a Makerspace in your school. Whenever you're given the choice between being you and being Batman, always choose Batman.

There are many more gadgets that you can find and place in your Makerspace, but I suggest checking them out online and reaching out to people on Twitter to see how they feel about them. Many blogs have reviewed the gadgets and can point you in the right direction based on your specific needs.

Just like teaching in the classroom is about the pedagogy first and the technology that supports it, the same is true for Makerspaces. What students want to learn and make always comes first, and they find the tools that support their interests.

I want to remind you one more time that a Makerspace isn't about the gadgets that are in it; it is about the ideas. The tools are a way for students to explore all the aspects of creating.

Maker Thoughts

List all of the things you would want to put in a Makerspace. Just go for it. Everything is fair game here!

_____

_____

_____

_____

_____

_____

_____

_____

_____

_____

_____

_____

_____

_____

_____

_____

Nerdy Work

Go searching the Internet and find
different ways that you can use some
of those awesome gadgets you wrote
down above. Think about how you would
use them, and if you can find awesome lessons,
then they might be perfect for your space. If not, you
might not need them as much as you think.

_____

_____

_____

_____

_____

_____

_____

_____

_____

_____

_____

_____

_____

EXTRA NOTES

_____
_____
_____
_____
_____
_____
_____
_____
_____
_____
_____
_____
_____
_____
_____
_____
_____
_____
_____
_____
_____

6

Makerspaces and Project-Based Learning

By now, you have an understanding of what Makerspaces are and what you can put in them, but how can you really use them? I would love to give an example of how you could use Makerspaces for every content area, but I'm not a teacher of every content area. I'm an English and social studies teacher. While I may not provide you a specific example of how to work in the Pythagorean theorem, cellular mitosis, or infinite improbability drives, I can talk about the big ideas that will fit into any curriculum to help teachers get the most out of Makerspaces.

Project-Based Learning

I have been a PBL teacher for a number of years now. I gradually moved away from the bubble tests until they were altogether eliminated from my classroom. It's been a freeing experience, but one that took time to achieve. Students will learn while working on assigned projects and demonstrate understanding through the creation of the final project. I'm sure there are plenty of fancy definitions out there, but that is the one I use. There are different ways to approach PBL, and I think I've done them all.

The Recipe

This is the standard PBL concept. This is where I started because I had no other idea where to start. With "The Recipe," a teacher gives a student or group of students a set format for the project. The instructions are detailed, and the student needs to follow the directions specifically to earn all of the points for the project. At the end of the unit, the teacher receives nearly identical projects from everyone in class. The teacher grades them, acts slightly annoyed that they're all the same, and they're passed back. Students jump through all of the hoops and are ready to move on to the next unit.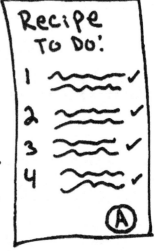

"The Recipe" is a natural starting place for teachers to figure out PBL (especially for those who are afraid to give up assignment control to the students). I've been there and I get it. You shouldn't live in this place very long though. Having students spit out exactly what you told them isn't real thinking. It's just reading directions and doing what they were told. It's compliance, and that is boring. We want students to take what they're given and have the freedom to create something new and exciting.

Special shout out to Chris Lehmann for first talking about the recipe concept. He has great books out there and you should buy them.

Nerd Alert

Some of the best things in the nerdy world were created by not following the rules. Joss Whedon is a nerd icon. He is popularly known for his work he has done with the Avengers. He brought those comic book heroes to the big screen in a way that has made over a billion dollars. However, it was the way he broke from the "traditional" way of things that made him a genius.

Whedon turned a valley girl stereotype into a vampire slayer who empowered thousands of girls around the country. A strong female lead in an hour-long drama that featured fight scenes was practically unheard of at the time. The scripts were funny, thoughtful, and creative. Sci-fi isn't filled with super strong female leads, and Whedon made sure to make his mark with Buffy. For fun, he wrote a musical episode for Buffy and it was amazing. It earned an Emmy nomination. He seemed to relish doing something he was told could not be done.

He also made waves with his *Dr. Horrible's Sing-Along Blog* musical Internet short. Doing shows exclusively on the Internet is now commonplace, but at the time, it wasn't a regular medium for new media. Add in that this was a musical, and it's something that would never regularly make the airwaves. Well, Dr. Horrible became an Internet darling and was later broadcast in its entirety on TV. With millions of views on YouTube, Dr. Horrible is a great example of how the Internet can be a place for new types of creativity.

Whedon could have easily chosen a male lead for his vampire drama or waited to get his musical short on TV, but he chose another route. He wanted to be different because he had a vision. That creative spirit drove him to do different projects and we all benefit from that.

Open Presentation Projects

This is not the OPP of my youth by Naughty by Nature. This OPP is another way to allow students some freedom in PBL. This is a step closer to full freedom for students, but still allows the teacher some control over the content. We all need to take baby steps, and this an excellent way to get there. Students are still given a specific set of directions but also the option to share these projects during the presentation. They could use a movie, puppet show, photography, metal sculpture, etcetera. The students have an opportunity to share what they learned and demonstrate understanding through a medium of their choosing that plays to their strengths. It's a wonderful way for a teacher to let students shine in class who might otherwise wilt under the pressure of a traditional, and very boring, slide show.

"But Nick, what if the students just make movies over and over again? Are they really learning?"

I tell students that once they use a particular medium, that medium is banned from future use for the semester or year. I do this to encourage students to push themselves to explore other presentation methods and because I don't want to see the exact same movie over and over again.

Open presentation projects are a great stepping stone to the next type of project, and teachers should look at multiple ways for expanding the freedoms of students when it comes to projects. A little bit of freedom for students can go a long way in the classroom.

Free-Range Projects

This is the biggest and scariest change for teachers when it comes to PBL. This is pure PBL. I call it free range because the students have the complete freedom to tackle any aspect of the unit that stands out to them. With this format, students are given a broad task and create the project and the rubric with the teacher's guidance. The students take ownership of all aspects of the project from beginning to end and dive deep into the area that they find most compelling. Student engagement goes through the roof and the students have the most fun. Here is just one example of how I have used it in my classroom.

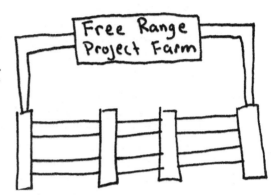

From the Nerd Files:

FRPs are my favorite part of class with my students. I always get the most inventive and interesting projects. After reading *The Great Gatsby*, I assigned an FRP and allowed the students free choice. The goal of the project was to adequately discuss one theme, one symbol, and two characters from the text. I always give students class time to work on the projects and I walk around providing guidance. I help students with their rubrics and point them in a direction if they get lost in the text or the analysis of a portion of the story. My role is to be the "guide on the side," as people like to say. I've done this style of project with my students for a number of years and I love the cool and different projects they have created. This year was no different. ▶

(Nerd Files continued)

A group of four students created an epic rap battle between Tom, Daisy, Gatsby, and Nick. The students wrote all of the lyrics, recorded their tracks, and one of the students created the beats for the song. It was amazing! The students spent time working on rhyme scheme and coming up with similes and metaphors to use in their songs. They rehearsed and supported one another as they worked on their lyrics. They made a video, too—met with great applause and a huge smile from me. Here is a link to the video (http://goo.gl/blaWUc) if you want to see their amazingness.

When we watched the video in class, a great discussion followed about the different aspects of the song and how they applied to the story. It was great to see these students all engaged in the symbolism, theme, and characterization of *The Great Gatsby*, and it all started with giving my students a chance to share their thoughts in a project of their choosing. As teachers, we want students to engage with the material and make it their own. This has been the best way to accomplish anything with my students.

Here are a few more examples of my awesome students doing awesome things that are worth checking out.

Interpretive Dance (https://goo.gl/V5mr52)

Gatsby Graffiti Project (http://goo.gl/Iu9Ksm)

The Sims (https://goo.gl/husztg)

Original Song for Gatsby (https://goo.gl/apKiwq)

This is something I never could have created for my students. It would have been terribly unfair for me to create a lesson that required students to rap with one another for a class project. Not everyone has those skills. We need to let students use the skills they have to show who they are. Buffy Summers didn't slay demons the way the Watcher's Council wanted her to, but she's the most successful slayer in history. Focusing on the strengths of the students to demonstrate understanding will always lead to successful learning objectives, and other fancy educational word things as well.

20 Time/Genius Hour

Twenty Time/Genius Hour is taking PBL to the extreme. It takes the FRP idea and expands it further. For 20 Time/Genius Hour, you give students class time to explore something they're passionate about. That is the basic skeleton. As a teacher, you can add any caveats you want, but the general outline is still the same. Kids explore their interests in class. The reason for the two different names is based on how you implement it in your classroom.

As a high school teacher, I called it 20 Time because I gave students 20% of the class week to work on their project. Every Friday was 20 Time, and students worked on their projects all class. I didn't take a single day away from them and they did some amazing things. I added my own aspects of 20 Time to focus on some curriculum-based items. I had students blog every other week about their project and they had to give a TEDx style talk at the end of the year that focused on what they learned, not what they did. For lower grades, most call it Genius Hour because they can sometimes dedicate an hour a day to those specific projects.

Some people think that the teacher's job during 20 Time/Genius Hour is to sit and watch kids work. Feet propped up and reading the newspaper is how some people envision 20 Time/Genius Hour unfolding. Honestly, that is how many people view all PBL. Nothing could be further from the truth.

If you're doing it right, you're busier on 20 Time/Genius Hour days than any other day because you're bouncing from student to student and group to

20 Time Rulz!!

group helping them with their work. Guiding students during 20 Time/Genius Hour and any other PBL takes time and effort. I have logged more miles on those days than any other day of the week. At times, the teacher needs to be the cheerleader and co-problem solver. With the right nudging, a student can go from a project failure to a huge success. The teachers are more important than ever in all PBL, but it really stands out during 20 Time/Genius Hour.

Nerd Alert

A great example of the "guide on the side" is *Buffy the Vampire Slayer*. According to the opening credits:

"Into every generation a slayer is born: one girl in all the world, a chosen one. She alone will wield the strength and skill to fight the vampires, demons, and the forces of darkness; to stop the spread of their evil and the swell of their number. She is the slayer."

Her job is to kick demon butt and save the world every episode. To do this, she needs someone to watch after her. That is why the Watchers Council was formed, to support the slayer in saving the world over and over again. Giles was her watcher, and he worked hard to train her in everything she needed, but she was resistant to the "traditional" methods of slaying. It wasn't until Giles learned to take a step back and teach Buffy based on the things she was learning on her own did their relationship solidify and Buffy grew as an individual. This guidance that Giles provided from the sidelines—and sometimes on the frontlines of the fight when he needed to model good slaying—was helpful in Buffy learning how to protect the citizens of Sunnydale. If Giles had not adapted his instructional methods, it's very likely that we would all be living inside the Hellmouth.

If you're thinking about 20 Time or Genius Hour, the names really don't matter. It's giving the students the freedom to explore their own passions that truly matters here. It's that freedom that promotes learning and allows for student growth. 20 Time/Genius Hour also validates what kids are excited about, and they love sharing that with others in the school setting.

Here are some of my student talks from our TEDxGrossePointe SouthHS event. They shared what truly mattered to them and I love sharing it with others. These are just a few of the videos that show the power of PBL at its finest.

- Kitty McKay - The Road to Mt. Kilimanjaro - (https://goo.gl/SsuLwP)
- Lucy Stonely - Portraits of a Bankrupt City - (https://goo.gl/aKnjYe)
- Miranda Berry - Don't Say What If, Say Why Not - (https://goo.gl/lNxyW0)
- Hannah Connors - Our Generation Will Prove Everyone Wrong - (https://goo.gl/MxK0G3)

Project-Based Learning and Makerspaces

Using PBL in a Makerspace can be done easily with the correct mind-set. PBL is about giving students options to explore things they're passionate about and demonstrate that understanding in various ways.

Makerspaces are about giving students access to tools that allow them to explore their passions in different ways. The two are meant to be together. As a teacher, you just need to point students to the Makerspace and have them use the tools to create some amazing projects. This might involve them using the green screen to create a film version of the short story "A Rose for Emily," 3D design and print a replica raft that Huck Finn used to make his way down the Mississippi River, or use a Raspberry Pi and Arduino to create a functional green light for *The Great Gatsby*. Every content area has the ability to come up with creative projects that allow students the freedom to explore areas that interest them. It's not going to be easy, but we didn't expect teaching to be easy.

A Makerspace is designed to support those exact types of projects. If schools want to create and grow a culture of Making, they need to allow students the freedom in the curriculum to Make. Teachers need to become more comfortable in turning over certain aspects of the class to the students. Once they do, creation, innovation, Making, and in-depth learning can take place.

Now that I have covered what the different types of PBL are, it's up to the expert to integrate that into the classroom. Don't look around or wait for someone to tell you what to do. You are the expert! You're always the expert of your classroom, and don't let others tell you any different. You know how to best work with those students and how to implement new ideas. I could never walk into your room and do what I do with my students. It would be an utter disaster. Take some of these ideas, tweak them, make them your own, and see how they fit in your class structure. You might find that it only takes a couple of tweaks for one class and a whole new approach with another. You will make the best decisions for your class, and I trust you to do it because you're an expert and a professional.

Nerd Alert

One of the greatest television shows in the world has to be *Saved by the Bell*. I have written extensively about how amazing it is and why every human who walks the earth should watch every episode. Twice. For educators, SBTB is a must watch if you want a solid understanding of PBL and how it impacts student learning. ▶

(Nerd Alert continued)

No matter what I write, I won't do justice to my TV childhood hero, Zack Morris. He was everything a young kid wanted to be. He was cool, dated the hottest girl in school, had an awesome phone he carried around, and was involved in crazy schemes that always seemed to work in his favor. As a high school student, I realized how silly everything he did was and that Bayside was not a "real" high school. When I study Zack, I see a student who really responded to one type of learning over all others. Zack was a PBL. Whether it was Buddy Bands, Screech's Spaghetti Sauce, the school pond that was damaged in an oil spill, or the host of other projects he was involved with, Zack excelled. Those lessons allowed Zack to dive into the material and create using ideas he was passionate about. The classes he hated the most were the ones where he needed to sit at his desk and take notes. Not being able to collaborate with his peers was the worst way to reach Zack.

I look at Zack and I see his silliness in students today. When I moved away from lecture-based lessons and started using more PBL, I saw an increase in student participation across the board. Kids were excited to be part of the learning. Working with their peers gave them a chance to show off their knowledge to others. Isn't that what Zack was really doing? He needed a chance to show others that he wasn't the goofball everyone thought he was. With a little structure, Zack could have created some amazing school projects. Belding tried very hard to harness Zack's energy by giving him chances to create things for the school. The video yearbook is a good example. The school store is another. KKTY is yet another example. When Zack was given a chance to really show what he was made of, he came through. Granted, he made calendars of the swim team and used the video yearbook as a dating service, but he helped set the radio station up to save The Max (with Slater's help) and exposed the sexism in Bayside's wrestling program. ▶

(Nerd Alert continued)

Think about the students in the classroom who are like Zack Morris. Are teachers writing those students off as silly kids who just need to calm down? Have I dismissed a student because he didn't fit my idea of a student years ago? Many people forget that Zack nearly aced his SAT. He was not a dumb student; instead, he was a student looking for the right motivation. When a teacher gave him the chance to shine, he did. Students like Zack usually go on to do amazing things when they get out of the educational system and are free to explore what they are passionate about. Let's not make those students wait until after high school or college. Let's give them a chance to be Zack now before it's too late. I never thought I would say this, but I would take a class full of Zacks over a class full of Jessies or Screeches any day.

Maker Thoughts

What was your favorite classroom project you
were given in school? Do you give the same type
of assignments to your students?

_____

_____

_____

_____

_____

_____

_____

_____

_____

_____

_____

_____

_____

_____

_____

_____

_____

_____

Nerdy Work

I want you to create an awesome
meme about PBL in the classroom.
Do your best sketch below and make a
meme. I double dog dare you to share
it on Instagram, Twitter, and Facebook
using #PBLMeme so we can all find it.
Come on, everyone else is going to be doing it.

7

Failure and Makerspaces

Like all things in education, teachers need to be open to failure. Makerspaces are the perfect space for students and educators to try new things and fail big time. Makerspaces are designed for experimentation. They allow for people to get ideas, try them out, and see what happens. Every single project I have seen in the Makerspace has had an aspect of failure. Schools need to help remove the stigma that's attached to failure, and Makerspaces are a wonderful place to start.

Failure isn't fun. Failure stinks and is a huge pain in the butt. We have all spent countless hours on various lesson plans that have blown up in our faces during class. It's how we react to those failures that speaks to who we are as educators. The same is true for students in Makerspaces. We need to make sure that the culture of failing and trying again is part of the space. Students are not new to failure. They experience it every day in an atmosphere that is accepting of it. We should all be proud of our failures and wear them as a badge of honor.

Nerd Alert

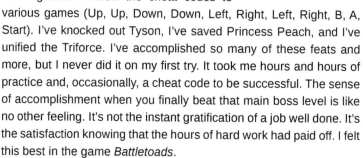

I have spent innumerable hours playing video games. I know the cheat codes to various games (Up, Up, Down, Down, Left, Right, Left, Right, B, A, Start). I've knocked out Tyson, I've saved Princess Peach, and I've unified the Triforce. I've accomplished so many of these feats and more, but I never did it on my first try. It took me hours and hours of practice and, occasionally, a cheat code to be successful. The sense of accomplishment when you finally beat that main boss level is like no other feeling. It's not the instant gratification of a job well done. It's the satisfaction knowing that the hours of hard work had paid off. I felt this best in the game *Battletoads*.

If anyone knows anything about *Battletoads* for NES (Nintendo), it's that the flying surfboard level is one of the hardest video game levels ever created. My brothers and I spent weekend after weekend trying to solve the puzzle. We would get a bit closer, but still had no idea how to crack it. Without the Internet, we were stuck comparing notes with friends at school and poorly written notes on scrap paper. Then, one glorious day, I beat that level. Everything seemed to click and I was able to do it. It was amazing. My older brother had not beaten it, but I had. It stands, to this day, as the height of my gaming accomplishments.

I have played many other video games and the easy ones bore me. There is little joy in doing something so easy. The difficult tasks bring the greatest joy. The harder the task, the more joy that can be found when it is completed well. This is true for the students in our classes today. We cannot let them shy away from the tough things. With our support, they will master various difficult skills, and feel better when they are done. Whether it's *Battletoads* or algebra, we want students to strive and overcome difficulty.

I can throw the trendy terms *grit* or *rigor* (or whatever is fancy right now) to explain why this is all important, but I don't think it's necessary. Hard work in doing something I was passionate about paid off with a wonderful sense of accomplishment. It took multiple failures to get to that point and I was OK with that. Our students aren't much different than we were growing up. They have things they're passionate about and they will try over and over again until they get it. It might be video games, but it also might be the guitar, shooting a basketball, or Making the perfect cupcake. Every student knows what it's like to fail and try again, but schools spend too much time chastising students for failing. Makerspaces are perfectly designed to combat that trend. Makerspaces allow students to try and fail and try again. With this in mind, students will become better problem solvers and critical thinkers because they have a background in failing. Makerspaces have the ability to help foster a generation of failures, and education needs to embrace that idea.

Maker Thoughts

What has been one of your biggest classroom failures? What did you do about failing so epically? Feeling bold? Share it with your students. Double bold? Share it with other teachers? <gasp>

Nerdy Work

Design a little card that you can give to all of your students that allows them to fail. Make it as awesome as you can, and then make copies of it and give it to them. Remind them that failing is part of the process, and that we all do it while trying to learn.

EXTRA NOTES

8

Final Thoughts

I wasn't sure what I was going to put in this chapter, but it would drive me nuts to have an odd number of chapters for some reason, so I figured some final thoughts might be good to tie everything together.

- If you want to put together a Makerspace, the best thing you can do is just get started. Too many things in life are planned and super organized. Just pick a day and start planning. Talk to students, parents, staff, the Internet, your personal Happy Hogan, and get the Makerspace going.
- Look around the Internet for how others have put together a Makerspace. Check out the tag #MakerEd for wonderful tweets that will provide some good tips, lessons, and other Makerspace goodies to inspire you as you go on your journey.
- Document what you do and share. The Maker community is as awesome as it is because we all share what we're doing. Nobody does this on their own, so giving back is the best way to say, "Thanks!" after using so many great ideas.
- Be OK with screwing up. You're going to make mistakes. It will model screwing up for your students, and being a screw up is generally one of the first steps toward being a success.
- It's fine to look at the fun toys that Makerspaces have to offer. Tools are great, and we all want to play with new tools, but

remember the space needs to be about what the students want/ need to Make, not what tools we can give the kids and make them use because we spent a chunk of money on them.

■ Try your hardest to find a spot for your Makerspace that is accessible to everyone on a regular basis. Makerspaces should bring people together, not drive them apart.

■ Make students part of the process. They will have a sense of ownership if they help design and build the space, and it will help grow the space organically if students are working to fill it with amazing projects.

■ Don't just build a Makerspace; become a Maker. If you want students to get their hands dirty and make things, you better be prepared to make things as well. If you're willing to learn and try new things, your students will too.

■ Lastly, don't forget to have fun. Makerspaces should be a fun spot away from the traditional grind of the school curriculum where students can explore their passions with the freedom to screw up and try again. Hopefully, one day, all classes in school will be like mini-Makerspaces, but until then, make sure the Makerspace is the oasis in the testing, grade-driven desert of school.

There are plenty of other things I could have said about Making, but I wanted to make this a short book for those who are looking to get a space off the ground. Don't hesitate to reach out to me on social media (@TheNerdyTeacher) if you have more questions on putting together a space for your classroom or school. I hope that you have as much fun making your space as I did making mine. Good luck, and get Making!

Hugs and High Fives,
Nicholas Provenzano

> I'm just a guy, standing in front of an educator, asking them to love Makerspaces.

Maker Thoughts

Go back to the end of the introduction and look at all the stuff you said you knew? What have you learned by reading this book? Share below.

_____

_____

_____

_____

_____

_____

Nerdy Work

This is where you get to put together your ultimate Makerspace plan. Use these pages for everything you need to make the best and coolest Makerspace the world has seen. I'm talking MC Hammer pants cool. Epic.

Since you're still here, I thought I would give you some cool Maker projects to do with this book. Consider this the hidden track of this Makerspace book. Better yet, consider this book a Makerspace just for you. It's a book about Makerspaces that IS a Makerspace. This is Inception/Kramer-level stuff here.

Hack this book! I want you to think of a way to use this book in a way that I never conceived. This can be something crazy or something tiny and simple, but I want you to stretch your hacking muscles in fun and creative ways. When you've hacked the book, please take a picture and share it on Twitter, Facebook, and Instagram, using the hashtag #ImAMaker.

On this page, draw something awesome. When you are done drawing something awesome, carefully rip the page out and flip it over.

Now, fold this paper origami-style into the picture you drew above. Sound impossible? Maybe, but give it a go! Share your work using #ImAMaker. (Thanks Jennie Magiera for the idea!)

Paper airplane time! This is your paper airplane sheet. Tear this out and go for it. Record a video and share your longest throw with the world. Tag it with #ImAMaker for all of us to find.

Nerd-flake! Take this piece of paper and fold it up. Cut out your favorite symbol of nerdiness like you would a paper snowflake. This will be your new favorite holiday decoration. Share it with #ImAMaker!

Design your own bow tie! Man or woman, bow ties are cool! You can use the next couple of pages to add some layers to your bow tie. Draw all the crazy designs you want and make the coolest bow tie in the world. As always, share it using #ImAMaker.

This one will require you to use almost every page of the book. Make a silly flip book using the corners of each page. Have something jumping, dancing, high-fiving, Making, or whatever. Record your very own animation and share using #ImAMaker

Turn this page into a thank you card for someone who has inspired you to be the amazing educator/Maker that you are. This could be another educator, a student, your own child, or Master Yoda himself. Saying thank you can make someone's day, so why not do it with a personalized note from a Makerspace book?

Find something that has meaning to you that connects to your Maker journey. Take a picture of it, tape the picture to this page, and draw/write around it words that stand out to you when you think about it. Share this with #ImAMaker.

Are you good at making hand puppets? Doesn't matter! You're going to turn this page into a tiny hand puppet. Make it look like you, your nemesis, or your favorite character from Star Wars that had like two seconds of screen time, yet everyone obsesses over for no really good reason. This character got an action figure so they could fill out Jabba's Barge. Or you know, whatever you want.

This is the end. The last sheet of paper is for you to create your very own Maker project and share with the world. Make sure to snap a picture or record a video and share it with the #ImAMaker tag for all of us to see.

I wouldn't be able to do all the crazy stuff I do without the most amazing people ever Made.

You're still reading?

It's over. Go to school.
Go. Buy a copy for a friend.

Start Making already.

(Bow bow, chick, chicka chicka)

Author Bio

Nicholas Provenzano is a passionate and nerdy teacher dedicated to giving every student a chance to learn something new and exciting. He has taught English language arts for 15 years but has always been a Maker. He has a master's degree from Central Michigan University in educational technology and has spent the past few years traveling the country and sharing the very cool things his students do in the classroom.

As a father, Nicholas loves spending time with his son as he explores the world around him. They love to laugh and play and Make things all the time. Everything Nick has accomplished though, is because of the support from his amazing wife. She is the real life Leslie Knope working to make the community a better place every day. She is way out of his league and he is very grateful she said yes.

At heart, Nick is a huge nerd who loves all thing pop culture: video games, movies, comic books, etcetera. These were things that were an important part of his childhood and he loves that he gets to share them with his son and the community on his website, TheNerdyTeacher.com, and his Twitter account, @TheNerdy Teacher. He looks forward to the next step in this crazy adventure and he hopes to meet all of you in his travels.

Work with Nick

Nicholas would love to visit your school, district or conference to share the great things he has learned with your staff. Nicholas has presented all over the country and would be happy to share about Makerspaces, PBL, Raspberry Pi, Genius Hour, digital tools to support reading and writing, Evernote, Google apps for education, and so many more topics related to technology and education.

If you're interested in bringing Nicholas in to visit, please send an e-mail to onenerdyteacher@gmail.com. I love meeting new people and sharing ideas. Reach out and we can make that happen.

CPSIA information can be obtained
at www.ICGtesting.com
Printed in the USA
BVOW06s2135251017
498687BV00007B/167/P